DAY OF THE DEAD
ORIGAMI

h

hinkler

hinkler

Published by Hinkler Books Pty Ltd
45–55 Fairchild Street
Heatherton Victoria 3202 Australia
www.hinkler.com

© Hinkler Books Pty Ltd 2017

Text, models & folding techniques © Matthew Gardiner or Steven Casey 2017
Paper designs © Shutterstock.com or Hinkler Books Pty Ltd
Images © Hinkler Books Pty Ltd or Shutterstock.com

Cover Design: Sam Grimmer
Cover Photography: Ned Meldrum
Internal Design: Aimee Zumis and Hinkler Design Studio

ISBN: 978 1 4889 0932 0

Printed and bound in China

CONTENTS

ABOUT THE DAY OF THE DEAD

The Day of the Dead, or *Día de Muertos* in Spanish, is a Mexican holiday to remember, honour and celebrate ancestors and family who have died. It occurs over two days, starting at midnight on 31 October and running until 2 November. Despite its name, the Day of the Dead is a joyous, festive family holiday filled with vivid colours, spectacular decorations, vibrant costumes, bright flowers and sumptuous food. For many Mexicans, it's a day of deep meaning, as well as a day to celebrate the joys of life.

Those who celebrate the Day of the Dead believe that the gates of heaven open at midnight on 31 October and the souls of children who have died (*angelitos*) return to visit their families on 1 November (*Día de los Inocentes*). They are joined by the spirits of deceased adults on 2 November (*Día de los Muertos*).

HISTORY

The festival originated in southern Mexico in pre-Hispanic times and is thought to be thousands of years old. It was originally a month-long celebration that occurred around July and August, toward the end of Mexican summer. The festivities honoured Mictlantecuhtli and his wife, Mictecacíhuatl—the Lord and Lady of the underworld (called Mictlan). With the arrival of the Spanish and the spread of Catholicism, over time the celebration moved to coincide with the Christian holidays of Halloween, All Saints' Day and All Souls' Day (31 October and 1 and 2 November).

FESTIVITIES

The Day of the Dead is celebrated across Mexico but is especially important in central and southern Mexico, where it originated. Families visit cemeteries where their loved ones are buried to clean and prepare the tombs for the arrival of the spirits. They make and decorate altars called *ofrendas* at the graves and sometimes in their homes.

The altars are festooned with candles, photos of the deceased, incense from the copal tree, religious imagery and flowers, and also with food and drink that people have prepared for the weary spirits to welcome them home. Toys and sweets are left for the spirits of children. It's a big family celebration of life: everyone gathers together at the graves to share food and drink, listen to music, sing and share tales about those who have passed on.

Many towns hold a parade (called a *comparsa*) with music and dancing. Locals carry an open coffin with a skeleton inside to the cemetery, like a funeral procession. People wear skeleton masks or make up their faces with dramatic skull designs and dress up in costumes and colourful clothes.

IMAGERY AND DECORATIONS

Many Day of the Dead decorations symbolise the four elements of nature: earth, water, fire and wind. Earth is represented by food and crops, water by the drinks left for the deceased, fire by the candles burning on the altars and wind by paper decorations (called *papel picado*). Perhaps the most recognisable image of the Day of the Dead festivities, though, is that of the decorated skull.

SKULLS AND SKELETONS

The decorated skull is called a *calavera* in Spanish. Edible skulls called *alfeñique* are made from sugar and are decorated with icing, beads and other embellishments. Other skulls are made from clay or wood as decorations. Calaveras are given to children as treats or toys and are also included as part of the altar ornamentation. Often the names of the deceased will be included as part of the decorations on the skull.

Another well-known Day-of-the-Dead symbol is the *calaca*: the figure of a skeleton. These are usually playful characters that are often depicted wearing traditional clothes, playing instruments, dancing and even getting married! In 1910, illustrator José Posada created a female character called *La Catrina* who has become a prominent part of the celebration. This elegantly dressed skeleton was originally called Lady Death and is thought to be linked to the Aztec goddess Mictecacíhuatl (the wife of Mictlantecuhtli, Lord of the underworld).

FLOWERS

Floral displays and offerings are an important part of the festivities, especially those featuring the Mexican marigold, called *cempasúchil*. This beautiful orange flower is placed on the altars for the dead and featured as artwork on the decorated skulls. The marigold is also known as *flor de muerto* (flower of the dead). Its distinctive aroma is thought to be a favourite of the spirits, attracting and guiding them back home. People will also scatter a trail of marigold petals from the cemetery to their houses for the spirits to follow.

Another popular flower is the bright purplish-red cockscomb (*barro de obispo*), which contrasts beautifully with the orange marigold. White flowers, such as baby's breath, are often used specifically for Día de los Inocentes on 1 November.

BUTTERFLIES

Ancient Mexicans believed that the spirits of the dead rested forever in the underworld (Mictlan), but that they could visit their descendants once a year. The annual migration of bright orange, white and black monarch butterflies (*mariposas*) occurs around the time of the Day of the Dead celebrations, with tens of millions of butterflies returning to Mexico from Canada in long, cloud-like flocks. These butterflies are thought to carry the returning spirits of the dead.

PAPEL PICADO

Rows of colourful *papel picado* (meaning 'cut paper' or 'pierced paper') are strung across streets and hung in plazas. These tissue-paper flags feature intricate designs consisting of a main figure or image against a window-pane-style background. Traditionally, these banners are made by master craftspeople who layer the sheets up to fifty at a time and use a chisel to cut a pattern into all of them at once. These flags are used at most Mexican celebrations, but the Day of the Dead papel picado are especially well known and feature skulls, skeletons and La Catrina. Those used on altars are often bright pink, orange or purple.

FOOD

Food plays a very important part in Day of the Dead celebrations and offerings. It is thought that spirits are nourished by the essence and aromas of foods, so families cook their deceased loved ones' favourite dishes and place them on the altars to attract their spirits home.

In addition to the sugar skulls, a special type of bread called *pan de muertos* (bread of the dead) features prominently in the offerings on the altars and as part of the festivities. There are several regional varieties, but the most common version is a round, sweet bread loaf sprinkled with sugar or sesame seeds. It is decorated with dough shaped in the form of bones and sometimes includes a teardrop representing the Aztec goddess Chimalma's tears for the living. Some regions also bake dark breads called *animas* (souls). These are shaped into humanoid figures and are left on the altars.

Food such as seasonal fruits, candied pumpkin and hot chocolate also commonly feature on the altars. Other popular foods include tamales (made of beans, cornmeal or meat wrapped in a banana leaf and steamed) and mole (a sauce made with chillies and chocolate).

Water and sweet drinks are left out to quench the spirits' thirst after their journey, and alcoholic drinks like tequila and mescal are provided on 2 November for the spirits of adults. Once the spirits are thought to have arrived, the family shares all the food in a celebratory meal.

ABOUT ORIGAMI

WHAT IS ORIGAMI?

Origami is a curious-sounding word because it is Japanese, not English, in origin. *Ori*, from the root verb *oru*, means 'to fold', and *kami* is one of the many terms for paper. In the purest renditions, origami creates an intended shape from a single sheet of paper with no cutting, gluing, taping or any other fastening device allowed. To create less rigid versions, one may make small cuts as in *kirigami* (cut paper), or long slits as in *senbazuru*—where a single sheet is effectively divided into a number of smaller, still-connected squares.

THE ORIGIN OF ORIGAMI

No one really knows when origami was invented. We do know that paper had to be invented first, so we can safely say that it is less than two thousand years old, but an exact date, even to the nearest century, cannot be authentically established. Despite its Japanese name, some claim that origami is Chinese in origin; this cannot be entirely discounted, since many art forms now claimed by others can be traced back to mainland China.

One reason for origami's hazy history is that for many centuries there was almost no documentation on how to do it. The oldest book known to contain origami-like instructions, the *Kanamodo*, is from the seventeenth century, yet older woodblock prints show paper folding. The oldest example of a book written about practising origami for entertainment is *Hiden Senbazuru Orikata* from 1797. The title, roughly translated, means 'the secret technique of folding one thousand cranes'.

There are around one hundred designs known as 'traditional origami' that were passed from person to person in Japanese culture, typically from a mother showing a child, or children sharing the knowledge among themselves. In fact, until the middle of the twentieth century, origami was thought of as something that women did as decorations for weddings, funerals and other ceremonial occasions, or something that young children did as a recreational pursuit.

After World War II, people from around the world started to visit Japan in greater numbers, and Japanese citizens increased their travel to other countries. Through this exposure, origami started to spread throughout the world, especially through exchange students—those young ambassadors of Japanese culture. The form began to spread across genders and cultures. Today, a finished model can be made and displayed for your own pleasure or given as a gift—cementing a friendship through paper folding.

In this book, you'll learn to create striking, colourful origami designs to use as Day of the Dead decorations.

HOW TO FOLD

By Matthew Gardiner

The key to high-quality origami is the quality of each fold. There are many kinds of folds, but the principles described here can be applied to most folds. Origami paper has a main side and an alternate side. When diagrams refer to the coloured side, it is to indicate the side (patterned/coloured) that you choose to be the dominant side in the final model.

1

Gently lift the bottom corner to the top corner. Don't crease yet; just hold the paper in position.

2

Line up the corners exactly. The corners in the image above are not aligned correctly.

3

The corners are exactly aligned; there is no visible difference.

4

Hold the corner with one hand, and slide the forefinger of the other hand down to the bottom.

5

Crease from the centre to the edge. Check that the crease goes exactly through the corner.

6

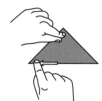

Crease from the centre to the edge on the other side to complete the fold.

In these two introductory folds, the edges and corners are the references. Use existing creases, corners, edges, intersections of creases and points to make sure your fold is accurate.

1

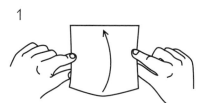

Lift the bottom edge to the top edge.

2

Align the corners and then align the edges on one side.

3

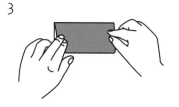

Align the opposite corner and edges so that both sides are perfectly aligned.

4

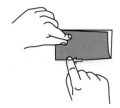

Hold one corner and crease from the centre to the edge.

5

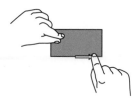

Crease from the centre to the other edge so all corners and edges are aligned.

SYMBOLS

By Matthew Gardiner

LINES

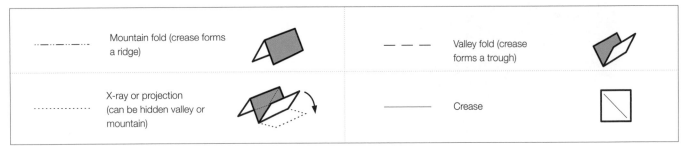

Mountain fold (crease forms a ridge)	Valley fold (crease forms a trough)
X-ray or projection (can be hidden valley or mountain)	Crease

ARROWS

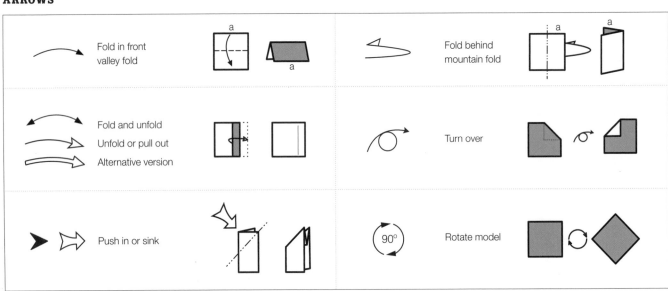

Fold in front valley fold	Fold behind mountain fold
Fold and unfold / Unfold or pull out / Alternative version	Turn over
Push in or sink	Rotate model

EXTRAS

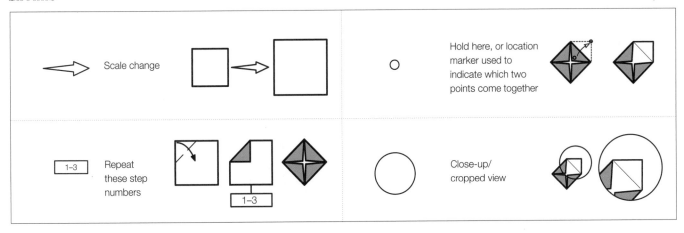

Scale change

Hold here, or location marker used to indicate which two points come together

1–3 Repeat these step numbers

Close-up/ cropped view

TYPES OF FOLDS

By Matthew Gardiner

BOOK FOLD

Valley fold one edge to another, like closing a book.

CUPBOARD FOLD

Fold both edges to the middle crease, like closing two cupboard doors.

BLINTZ FOLD

Fold all corners to the middle. This was named after a style of pastry called a blintz.

INSIDE REVERSE FOLD

The spine of the existing fold is reversed and pushed inside.

OUTSIDE REVERSE FOLD

The spine of the existing fold is reversed and wrapped outside.

PETAL FOLD
The petal fold is found in the base of the traditional origami crane and is used in some of these origami models.

1

Start coloured side up. Fold and unfold diagonals. Turn over.

2

Book fold and unfold.

3

Bring three corners down to meet bottom corner. Start with corners 1 and 2 together followed by corner 3.

PETAL FOLD Cont.

4

Fold top layer to the centre crease.

5

Fold and unfold the top triangle down. Unfold flaps.

6

Lift the top layer upward.

7

After step 3, the model is 3D. Fold the top layer inward on existing creases.

8

Completed petal fold.

SQUASH FOLD
A squash fold is the symmetrical flattening of a point. The flattening movement is known as squashing the point.

1

Pre-crease on the line for the squash fold.

2

Open up the paper by inserting your finger. Fold the paper across.

3

As you put the paper in place, gently squash the point into a symmetrical shape.

4

Completed squash fold.

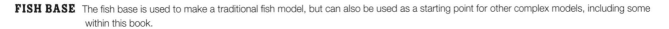

FISH BASE The fish base is used to make a traditional fish model, but can also be used as a starting point for other complex models, including some within this book.

1

Start with white side up. Fold and unfold diagonal.

2

Fold both sides to the middle.

3

Mountain fold in half behind.

4

Squash fold both sides.

5

Mountain fold the back layer behind.

6

Completed fish base.

WATERBOMB BASE Origami has standard shapes that are often repeated because they are very useful. The original use of this base form was to make a waterbomb model, but its five points make a versatile shape for many designs.

1

Begin coloured side up. Book fold and unfold. Turn over.

2

Fold and unfold diagonals.

3

Collapse on existing creases.

4

Completed waterbomb base.

PLEAT

Fold alternate mountain and valley lines, one over the other.

KITE BASE

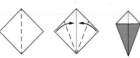

Crease the diagonal, then fold edges in to meet the crease.

SWIVEL FOLD

A swivel fold is often made on a pleat. It narrows its two points, and the excess paper swivels under one of the points.

17

SKULLS AND COSTUMES

SMILING SUGAR SKULL

Model: Matthew Gardiner
Diagrams: Matthew Gardiner

The sugar skull is perhaps the best-known symbol of the Day of the Dead. Add this origami skull to a greeting card, give it as a gift, or make lots to use as decorations for a Day of the Dead celebration!

1

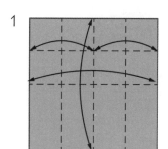

Fold in half, then in quarters as shown.

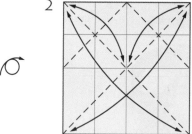

2

Fold diagonals. Fold top corners to the centre and unfold.

3

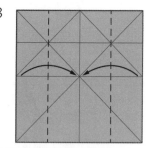

Cupboard fold edges to the centre.

4

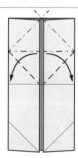

Squash fold along the marked mountains and valleys.

5

Fold the corners up to form the eyes.

6

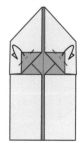

Mountain fold corners behind to shape the eyes.

SMILING SUGAR SKULL

7

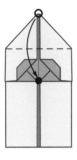

Fold the top corner down.

8

Valley fold corners outward to touch the edge. Mountain fold the top corners behind.

9

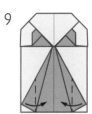

Valley fold the corners inward.

10

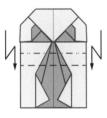

Pleat the top of the head downward to form the nose and cheeks.

11

Fold the bottom edge upward to form the mouth; see step 14. Turn over.

12

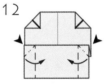

Squash fold on both edges.

13

Turn over.

14

Mountain fold the corners behind to shape the chin and cheeks.

15

This is the finished smiling sugar skull.

SUGAR SKULL

Model: Steven Casey
Diagrams: Steven Casey

This advanced origami skull is quite challenging, so make sure you master the previous simple origami skull first. With patience and practice, you'll find that this piece is well worth the effort!

1

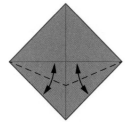

Coloured side up. Crease diagonals and fold bisectors in lower half.

2

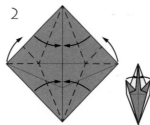

Add fish base creases, then collapse into a fish base.

3

Add angle bisectors.

4

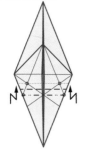

Add a pleat where indicated.

5

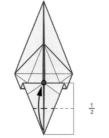

Fold the flap in half.

$\frac{1}{2}$

6

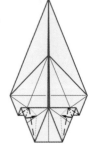

Swivel the lower edges inward.

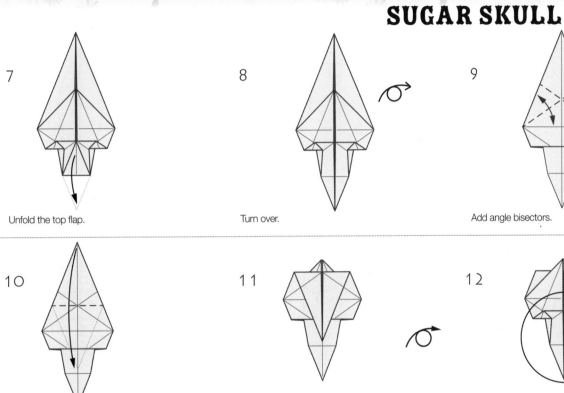

7

Unfold the top flap.

8

Turn over.

9

Add angle bisectors.

10

Fold through the folded intersection.

11

Turn the model over.

12

See detail in the following steps.

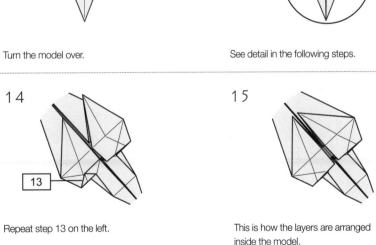

13

Bring one layer in front on the right.

14

13

Repeat step 13 on the left.

15

This is how the layers are arranged inside the model.

16

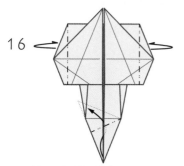

Mountain fold side flaps. Inside reverse fold up through the bottom layers.

17

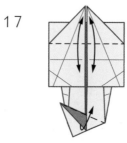

Fold and unfold the top flaps. Valley fold small flap upward.

18

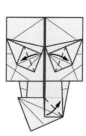

Valley fold flaps down so they touch the folded edge near the small crease. Fold the small edge down to the diagonal crease.

19

Valley fold top flaps up to the edge points. Fold small flap along the existing crease.

20

Squash fold the top flaps. Flip over the small flap and slip under the corner on the right.

21

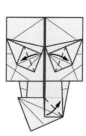

Fold over the flaps on the eyes. Valley fold small flap on the diagonal.

22

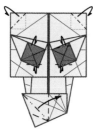

Fold top corners behind. Fold edges of eyes under. Swivel bottom flap to the right.

23

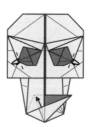

Pull out layers from pocket. Fold outer corner of eye sockets under.

24

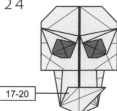

17-20

Mirror steps 17–20 on the left side.

24

25

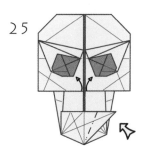

Reverse fold flap. Lift middle layers up.

26

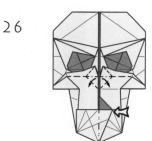

Reverse fold inner corners using
only the upper layer of paper.
Reverse fold flap.

27

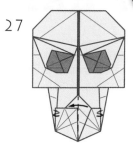

Fold flap over to the opposite side.
Place vertical edges under the
layers of the jaw.

28

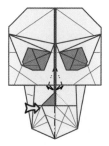

Tuck middle edges under. Reverse
fold left flap.

29

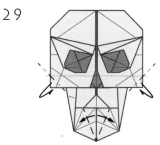

Fold corners behind. Fold middle
flaps along existing creases.

30

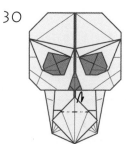

Mountain fold flap slightly under the
adjacent edges.

31

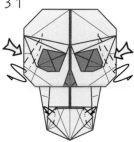

Crimp the sides at the top, so model becomes
slightly 3D. Tuck bottom corners under.

32

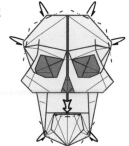

Add final shaping with mountain
folds. Shape mouth.

33

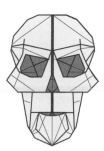

Completed sugar skull.

TOP HAT

Model: Matthew Gardiner
Diagrams: Matthew Gardiner

Many people include a top hat as part of their Day of the Dead costume. This origami top hat looks great when paired with an origami skull.

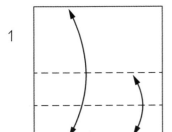

1

Fold in half horizontally. Fold the bottom quarter.

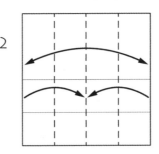

2

Fold in half vertically. Cupboard fold edges to the centre.

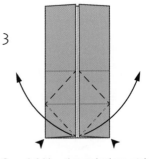

3

Squash fold on the marked mountains and valleys, lifting the corner outward.

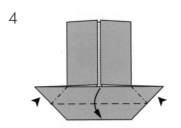

4

Squash fold along the marked mountains and valleys.

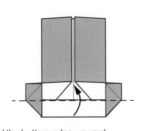

5

Fold the bottom edge upward. Turn over.

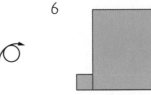

6

The finished top hat!

SOMBRERO

The word *sombrero* is Spanish for 'hat'. The wide-brimmed sombrero is ideal for the hot Mexican conditions and is known for being worn by cowboys and mariachi musicians. It also is a good accessory for your skull!

Model: Steven Casey
Diagrams: Steven Casey

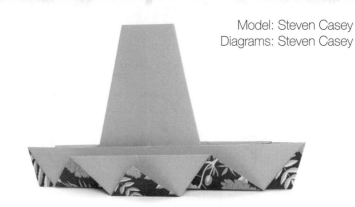

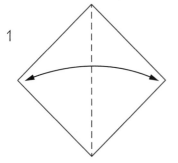

1

Fold and unfold diagonal.

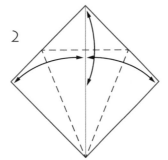

2

Crease kite base.

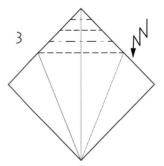

3

Add pleats to the top triangle.

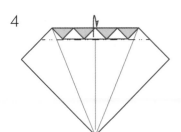

4

Mountain fold at the base of the pleats.

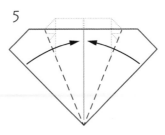

5

Fold the edges to meet the centre crease.

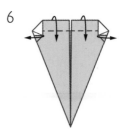

6

Fold the top edges down and squash fold the side points outward.

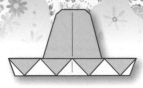

SOMBRERO

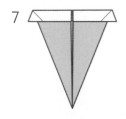

7

Your folds should look like this.
Turn over and rotate 180°.

8

Fold the top point behind. Make a
pleat at the bottom.

9

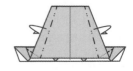

Swivel fold the edges to narrow
the peak of the sombrero.

10

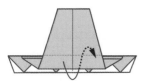

Tuck the pleat behind the brim.

11

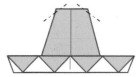

Shape the top with mountain folds.

12

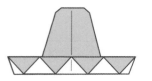

The finished sombrero. *Olé!*

BOW TIE

Model: Steven Casey
Diagrams: Steven Casey

An elegant bow tie complements any Day of the Dead costume! These origami bow ties look fabulous when made with geometrically patterned paper and bright colours.

1

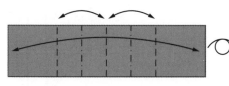

Use a 4:1 sheet. Fold in half, then quarters, then fold the middle to make eighths. Turn over.

2

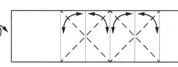

Crease the diagonals as shown. Turn over.

3

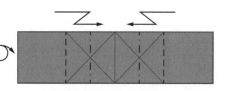

Pleat both sides inward.

4

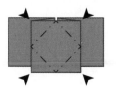

Reverse fold the corners.

5

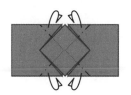

Mountain fold the corners behind.

6

Finished bow tie!

HEART

Model: Matthew Gardiner
Diagrams: Matthew Gardiner

This heart can be a decoration on the front of a Day of the Dead card or a Day of the Dead altar decoration. It can be made using A4 or letter paper.

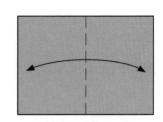

1

Book fold and unfold. Turn over.

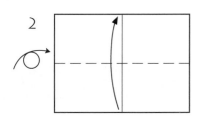

2

Fold in half lengthwise and unfold.

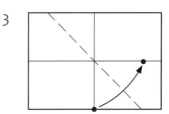

3

Valley fold a diagonal so that the vertical crease touches the horizontal crease.

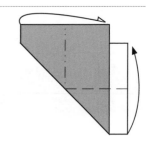

4

Fold the corners together, noting the mountain fold on the upper part and the valley fold on the lower part.

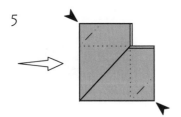

5

Inside reverse fold the points. The edge of the crease should match with the inner layer of the paper.

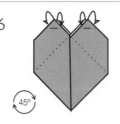

6

Rotate the model 45°. Fold the tips inside the heart.

7

Completed heart.

FLOWER CROWN

Model: Traditional / Matthew Gardiner
Diagrams: Matthew Gardiner

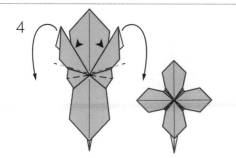

Flowers are used in all sorts of Day of the Dead decorations and costumes. Make this garland in traditional Day of the Dead colours, like orange, purple and white, or make a colourful crown with bright patterns.

1

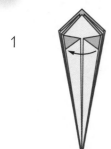

Start from step 9 of the iris origami piece on page 41. Fold the top layer across.

2

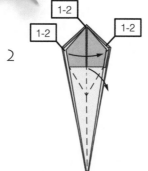

1-2   1-2   1-2

Fold the layer back, pulling out the point. Repeat on remaining three sides.

3

Fold the top petal downward.

4

Flatten the two side petals.

5

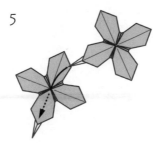

Make another iris and insert the stem from one iris into another.

6

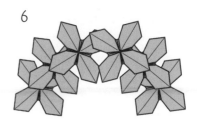

Make as many as you need to create your flower crown.

COMPOSITE SKULLS

Model: Matthew Gardiner

Pull together several origami pieces to make a variety of skulls that are full of individuality and charm. Try using different colours, patterns and costumes to see what personalities you can come up with. Use these characters to welcome guests to a Day of the Dead party, or send them as a themed greeting!

For the pieces of your composite skulls to be the right size in relation to each other, the skull needs to be made of paper measuring 200 × 200 mm (7 7/8 × 7 7/8 in.) and the bow tie paper should be 100 × 25 mm (4 × 1 in.). Hearts can be either smaller and made from 42 × 30 mm (2 × 1 3/16 in.) paper, or medium and made from 52 × 36 mm (2 3/64 × 1 27/64 in.) paper. The flower-crown flowers can be made of either 75 × 75 mm (3 × 3 in.) or 100 × 100 mm (4 × 4 in.) paper.

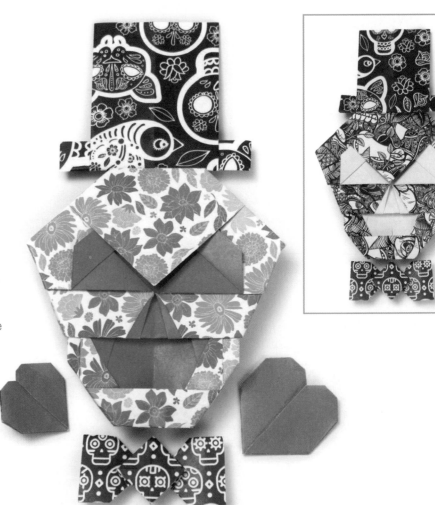

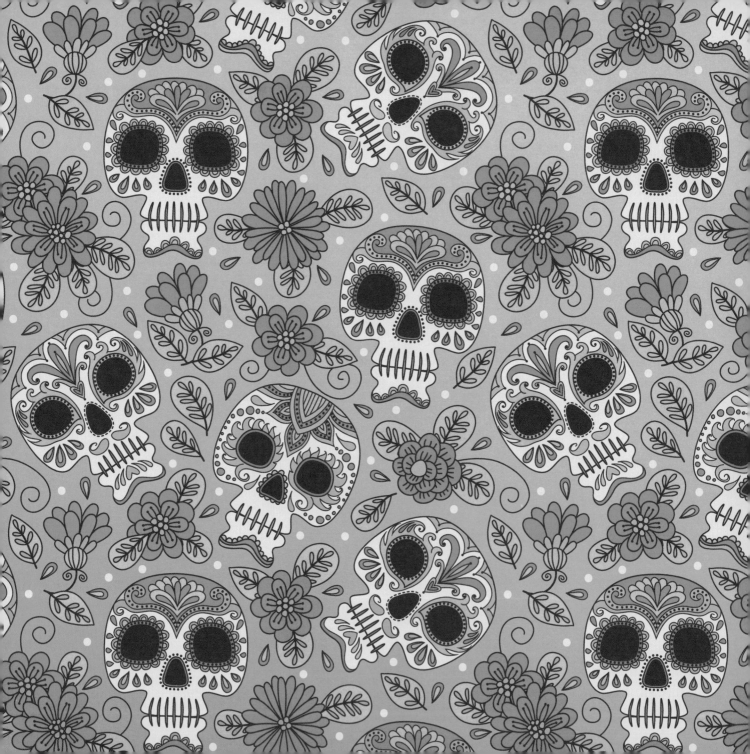

FLOWERS

MODULAR MARIGOLD

Model: Matthew Gardiner
Diagrams: Matthew Gardiner

The orange marigold is known as the *flor de muertos* ('flower of the dead') and festoons altars, paths and graves during the Day of the Dead festivities. This origami flower is made with several pieces and makes a stunning decoration.

1

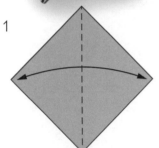

Fold in half diagonally.

2

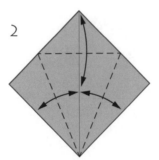

Fold the top corner. Fold edges to the centre.

3

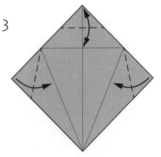

Fold top corner in half and fold side corners inward.

4

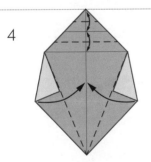

Fold edges to meet the centre crease. Fold top corner into quarters.

5

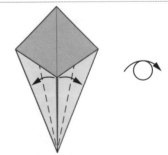

Fold the top layers in half. Turn over.

6

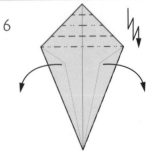

Pleat top corner. Fold out bottom layer from behind.

7

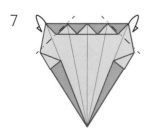

Mountain fold the corners behind.

8

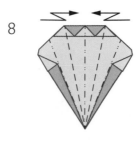

Pleat on diagonals inward from both sides.

9

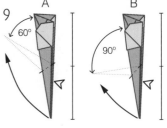

Two variations: A and B. Fold A to 60° and B to 90° with a reverse fold.

10

A and B. Insert the point of B into the slot fold of A. Rotate 90°.

11

Reverse fold the point in half. Fan out both petals.

12

Completed petal unit. Make four units to complete the marigold.

13

Let's make the receptacle (part that holds the petals). Fold diagonals. Turn over.

14

Valley fold all corners to the centre.

15

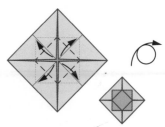

Fold inner corners three-quarters of the way to the edge. Turn over.

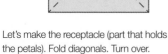
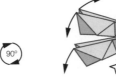
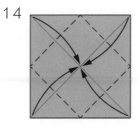

MODULAR MARIGOLD

16

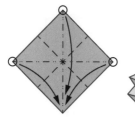

Collapse into a waterbomb base.

17

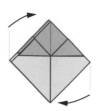

Fan out all the corners.

18

The completed marigold receptacle.

19

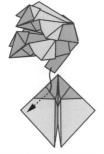

Insert the petals into the pocket of the receptacle.

20

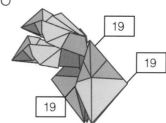

19

19

19

Repeat step 19 on all other points, inserting the petals into the receptacle.

21

All petals are inserted. Fold the four bottom points of the receptacle upward.

22

This is a side view showing the flat bottom.

23

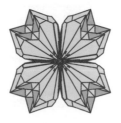

Top view of the completed marigold.

AZTEC-INSPIRED FLOWER

Model: Darren Scott
Diagrams: Darren Scott

This origami flower, with its geometric pattern of triangles, is reminiscent of Aztec art. This is an appropriate way to honour the ancient roots of this Mexican holiday, which is thought to be thousands of years old.

1

Start with the square coloured side up. Book fold.

2

Fold the front layer in half and unfold.

3

Fold the top left corner so it lies along the crease made in step 2 and unfold.

4

Sink the top left corner along the crease made in step 3.

5

Fold the top right corner down so it lies along the left edge.

6

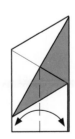

Fold the top layer to the left and unfold. This will be used to lock the units in place later.

AZTEC-INSPIRED FLOWER

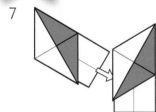

7

Insert two units together.

8

Fold to the left and tuck under flap. This locks the units together.

9

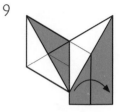

Unfold the lock. These will be refolded in steps 13 and 14.

10

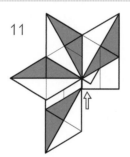

Add the third unit.

11

Add the remaining units.

12

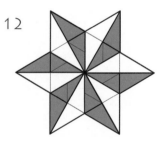

This will be the result. Now we need to lock the units in place.

13

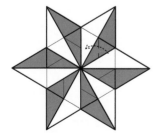

Refold the crease from step 9 to lock the units together.

14

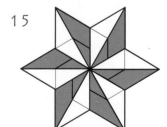

Lock the remaining units in place.

15

Completed six-point flower.

IRIS

Model: Traditional, Japan
Diagrams: Matthew Gardiner

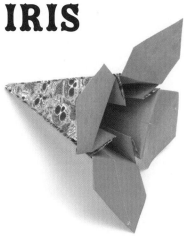

The iris takes its name from the Greek word for rainbow, reflecting the wide range of colours that appear in different species of iris. This model looks best when folded from blended or two-toned paper. It's a striking flower to add in appropriate Day of the Dead colours to your displayed bouquets!

1

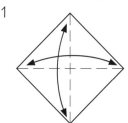

Fold and unfold diagonals.
Turn over.

2

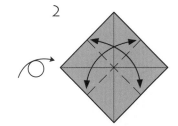

Book fold and unfold.

3

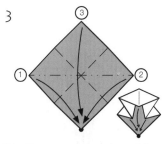

Bring three corners down to meet the bottom corner. Start with corners 1 and 2 together followed by corner 3.

4

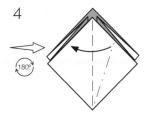

Rotate the model 180°.
Pre-crease, then squash fold.

5

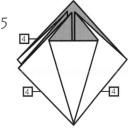

Repeat step 4 on the other three sides.

6

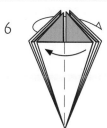

Turn top and back layers over.

IRIS

7

Fold top layer edges to meet the middle.

8

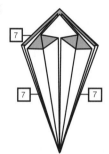

Repeat step 7 to both sides and behind.

9

Fold front petal down.

10

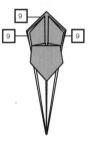

Repeat step 9 on all three sides, making the model 3D. Start with both side petals followed by the back petal.

11

Completed iris.

LILY

Model: Traditional, Japan
Diagrams: Matthew Gardiner

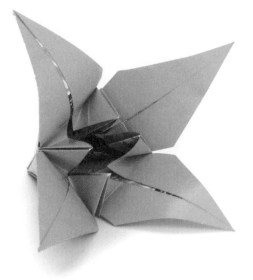

This piece continues on from the instructions for the iris up to step 7, but starts with the coloured side up. The lily is a flower widely associated with death. While not traditionally associated with the Day of the Dead, it makes a great piece to add to your Day of the Dead floral garlands.

1

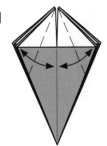

Start from step 7 of the iris. Fold the top layer only to the centre crease.

2

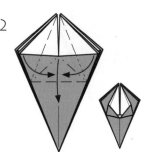

Petal fold; pull down the top layer and fold the sides to the middle. Lastly, make the mountain folds.

3

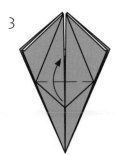

Completed petal fold. Fold the triangle flap upward.

4

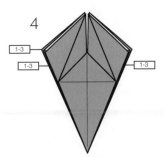

1-3
1-3
1-3

Repeat steps 1–3 on the three remaining sides.

5

Fold one layer in front and behind.

LILY

6

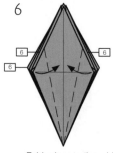

Fold edges to the middle, thinning the lily. Repeat on the other three sides.

7

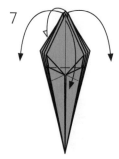

Make a soft, curved valley fold on all four sides to open out the lily.

8

Completed lily.

VERDI'S VASE

Model: Traditional, China
Diagrams: Mark Kennedy

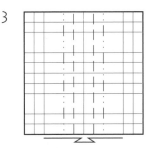

This vase was popularised in the United States by Verdi Adams, who taught it at the Origami Center of America. It is a fantastic model that produces a solid 3D form. Be careful when opening the model during the last steps so the paper doesn't crumple. Use it to decorate a Day of the Dead altar, and display your origami flowers within with the help of pipe-cleaners or craft sticks.

These diagrams were originally published in the OUSA Newsletter #34, Fall 1989. They are reproduced here with permission from Mark Kennedy.

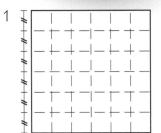

1 White side up. Crease into sixths in both directions.

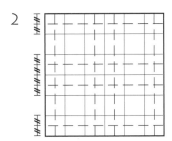

2 Crease in half the first, third, fourth and sixth 6ths in both directions.

3 On existing creases, pleat to the centre line.

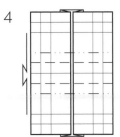

4 On existing creases, pleat to the centre line.

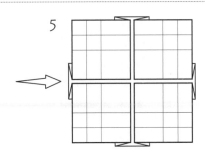

5 The model should look like this. Turn over.

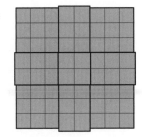

6 Completed step 5.

VERDI'S VASE

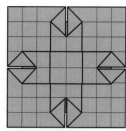

6A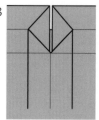

Pull down top layer while squashing in the sides.

6B

Squashes complete.

7

Moves completed on all four sides. Turn over.

8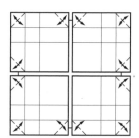

Pre-crease corners as shown to make step 11 easier.

9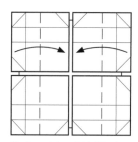

Cupboard door fold sides to the centre.

10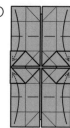

Cupboard door fold top and bottom to centre and tuck the corners into the pockets.

11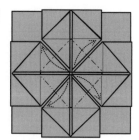

Cupboard door fold top and bottom to centre and tuck the corners into the pockets.

12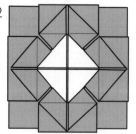

All folding is done. Turn over.

13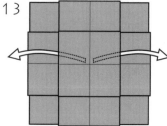

Start to open out vase by pulling out the extra layers along the sides. Be careful and work slowly.

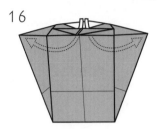

14

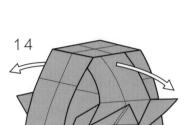

One pair of sides already pulled out.
Pull out the other side.

15

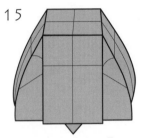

All sides are pulled out. Turn over.

16

Reach inside the top of the vase,
and poke out and round the
corners.

17

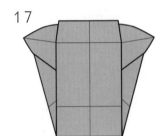

Completed vase—side view.

18

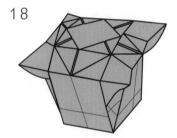

Completed vase—top view.

ORNAMENTS

SPANISH BOX

Model: Traditional, Japan
Diagrams: Matthew Gardiner

The traditional Spanish box was brought to the world origami stage by the British magician and origami expert Robert Harbin during his famous BBC television series, *Origami*. It's a practical decorative model, and if you use a 30 cm (12 in.) sheet or larger of stiff card you can create a strong vessel for candy and food at Day of the Dead parties.

The Spanish box is so named because of the decorative pleating on the rim of the box.

1

Fold and unfold diagonals.

2

Blintz fold.
Turn over.

3

Blintz fold again.

4

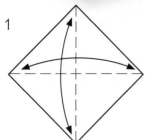

Fold top layers from the centre to corners.

5

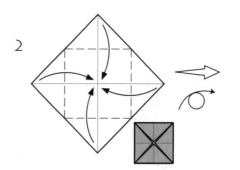

Completed step 4. Turn over.

6

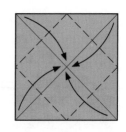

Fold top layers from the centre to corners.

7

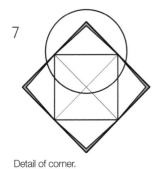

Detail of corner.

8

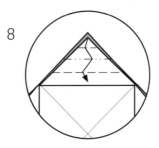

Fold over as shown.

9

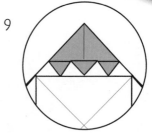

Completed step 8.

10

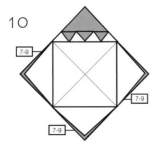

7-9

7-9

7-9

Repeat steps 7–9 on other three corners.

11

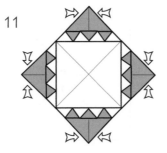

Pinch each corner as shown by the white arrows, making the box 3D.

12

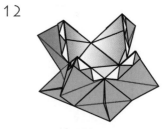

Completed Spanish box.

WENTWORTH DISH

Model: Nick Robinson
Diagrams: Nick Robinson

Nick Robinson has a penchant for creating simple paper dishes that have elegant forms and equally elegant paper locks. The finished shape of this Wentworth dish has variations that can be achieved by altering the angle of one fold. Use it as a dish for Day of the Dead parties or on an altar.

The dishes Nick Robinson is so fond of folding are inspired by the work of origami artist Philip Shen.

1

Fold and unfold.

2

Blintz fold. Turn over.
Rotate the paper 45°.

3

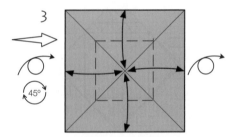

Fold and unfold edges to the centre as shown. Turn over.

4

Fold corners inside.
Turn over again.

5

Fold and unfold.

6

Fold the top layer to the left and unfold.

WENTWORTH DISH

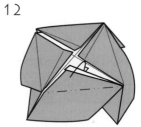

7

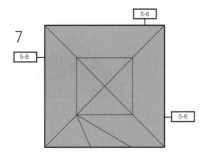

Repeat steps 5–6 on the other three sides.

8

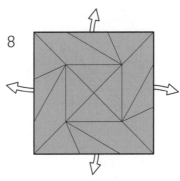

Unfold the sheet completely.

9

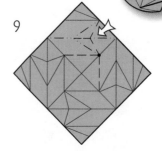

Sink fold. Make sure that the black dot goes down.

10

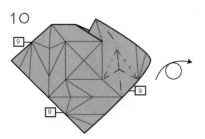

Repeat step 9 on the other three sides. Turn over.

11

To lock the bottom, fold up.

12

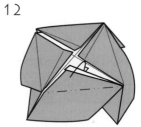

Tuck flap inside for a white centre.

13

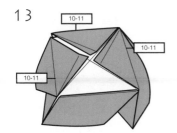

Repeat steps 10–11 on the other three sides.

14

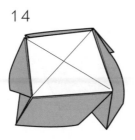

Completed back. Turn over.

15

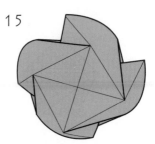

Completed dish.

CUP

The cup is a traditional model that actually works. Water and other liquids are always left out for the spirits during the festival.

Model: Traditional, Japan
Diagrams: Matthew Gardiner

1

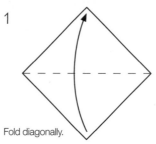

Fold diagonally.

2

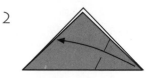

Fold corner to side. Notice that the top edge of the fold will end up parallel to the bottom edge.

3

 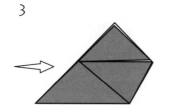

It should look like this. Turn over.

4

Repeat step 2 on the other side.

5

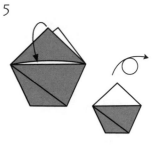

Slip top corner into pocket. Turn over.

6

Repeat step 5 with the remaining point.

7

Open up pocket.

8

Completed cup.

STANDING FAN

Model: Traditional, Japan
Diagrams: Matthew Gardiner

Table decoration is never complete without an origami-inspired napkin fold. The best results are achieved with an ironed napkin. For large napkins, you may find that adding more pleats in step 2 will make a more attractive fan. Use patterned paper to make a stunning Day of the Dead party decoration.

The standing fan napkin fold looks elegant on any table setting.

1

Fold in half.

2

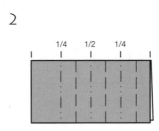

Accordion fold.

3

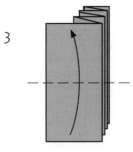

Fold up all layers.

4

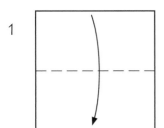

To make the stand, fold corners of both layers diagonally, tucking them under the accordion folds.

5

Push outward.

6

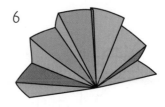

Completed standing fan napkin fold.

STRIPED CANDY

Model: Steven Casey
Diagrams: Steven Casey

Candy is an important part of a Day of the Dead altar, as it is especially left out for the spirits of children. Try making several candy origami pieces, then display them in one of your origami dishes!

1

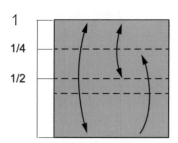

Fold in half, then add quarter crease in the top half. Fold the near edge up to top crease.

2

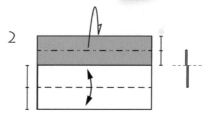

Mountain fold the coloured section behind. Crease the white section.

3

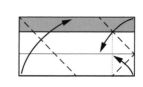

Valley fold the three corners.

4

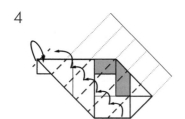

Fold over from the right, rolling over each step. Fold the tip over on the left. Rotate to step 5.

5

Tuck the flap into the inner pocket at the top.

6

Completed candy. Now, make some more candy for the bowl.

CHURRO

Churros are a doughnut-style treat that originated in
Spain. They are popular in many Hispanic countries,
including Mexico!

Model: Matthew Gardiner
Diagrams: Matthew Gardiner

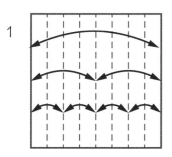

1

Fold in half, quarters, then eighths. Turn over.

2

Fold over top and bottom edges.

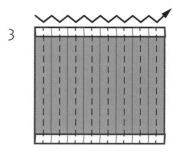

3

Valley fold pleats on 1/16ths.

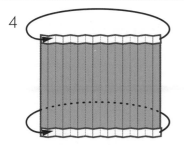

4

Roll up, and overlap by one 1/8th
section.

5

Tuck the overlap underneath the fold
at top and bottom.

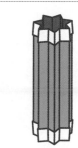

6

Complete! Make more to fill the
sweets bowl.

BUTTERFLY

Model: Traditional, Japan
Diagrams: Matthew Gardiner

Butterflies, or *mariposas*, are thought to guide the spirits home during the festival. Their delicate shape is perfect for hanging decorations. Use bold orange colours or try a detailed floral pattern.

1

Fold and unfold diagonals.

2

Book fold both ways.

3

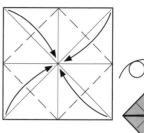

Blintz fold, then turn over.

4

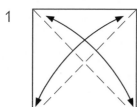

Blintz fold, then turn over.

5

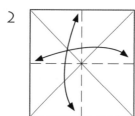

Completely unfold out to a flat sheet.

6

Fold sides to the middle.

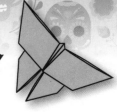

7

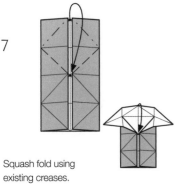

Squash fold using existing creases.

8

Repeat step 7 on the bottom.

9

Mountain fold in half.

10

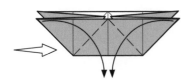

Fold points on the top layer down.

11

Fold sides in.

12

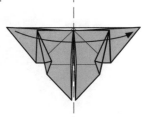

Fold in half.

13

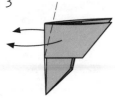

Fold both wings.

14

Fold one wing back.

15

Completed butterfly.

PAPER

In this section, you will find some handy paper squares with which to make your origami creations. For pieces that need rectangular paper, just trim the squares to the correct proportions.

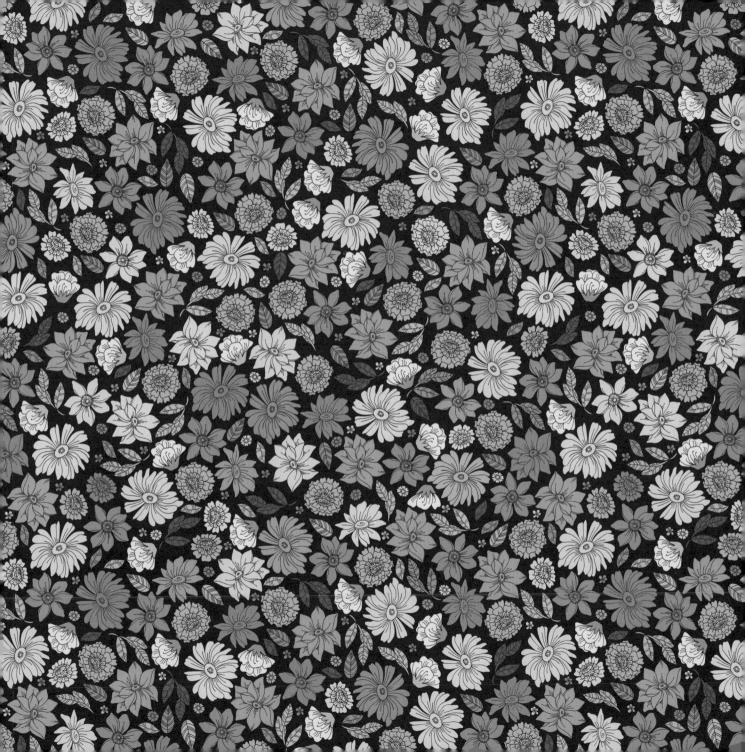

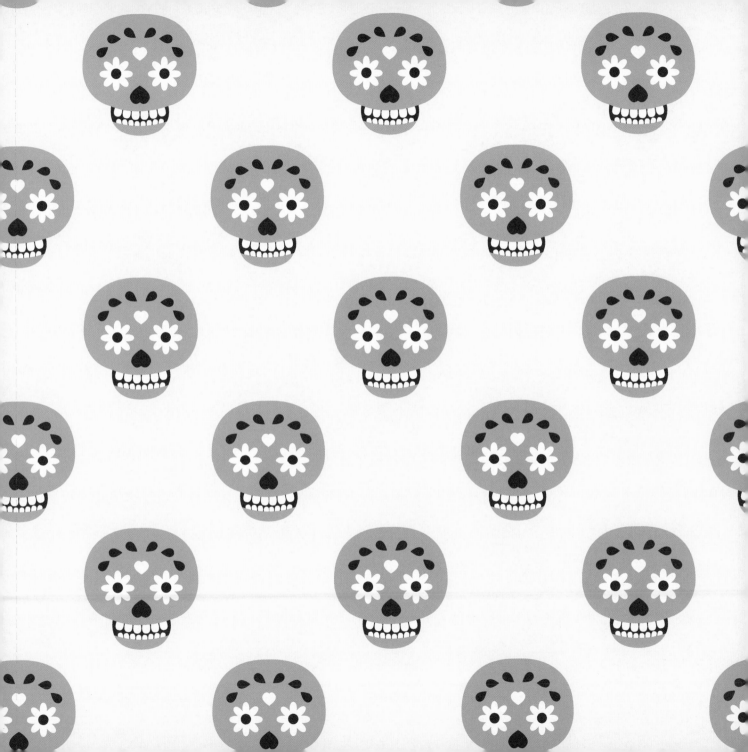

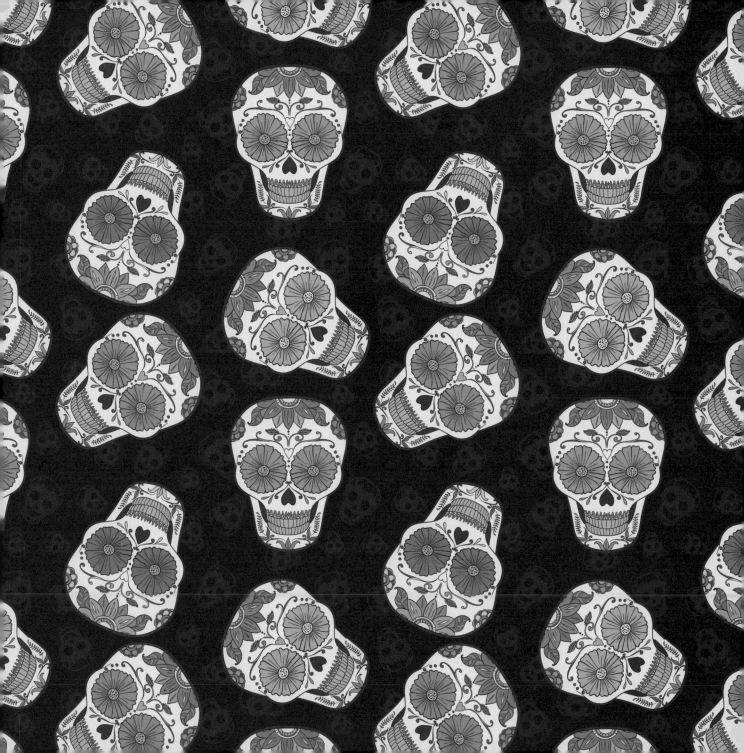

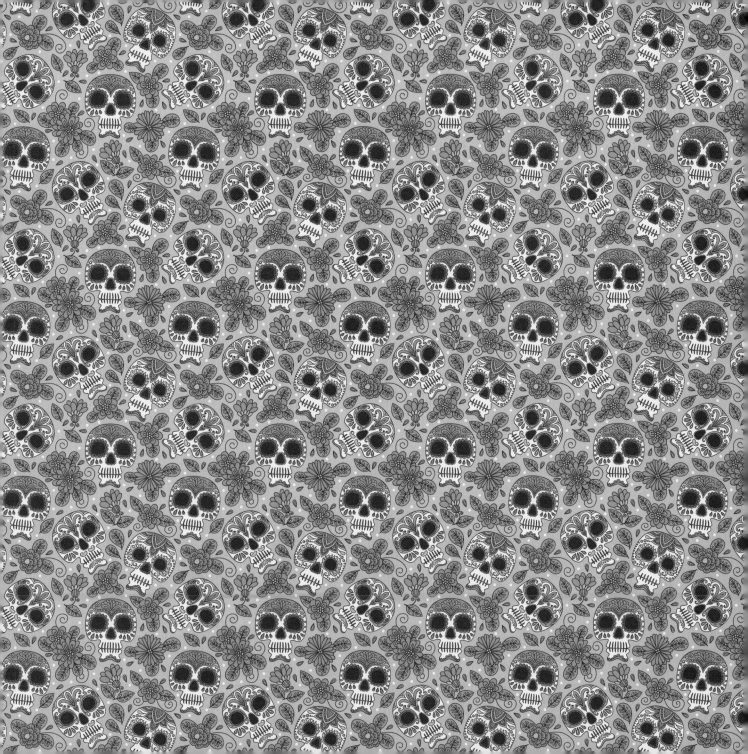